The Words Can Heal Handbook

How changing your words can transform your life and the lives of others

Hilary Rich   *Irwin Katsof*   *Chaim Feld*

Foreword by Jack Canfield

LEVIATHAN PRESS
Baltimore, Maryland

The Words Can Heal Handbook: How changing your words can transform your life and the lives of others

Text and graphics © 2002 by Words Can Heal, Inc.
Cover design © 2002 by Lightbourne

ISBN 1-881927-23-7
LCCN 2001092626

Leviathan Press
2505 Summerson Road
Baltimore, Maryland 21209

Printed in the United States of America

Editing: Helaina Kravitz, Uriela Obst,
          Lisa A. Smith, Elyse Green, Tamar Smith
Interior Design: Carla Martin
Interior Illustrations: Gary Val Tenuta
Cover Design: Gaelyn Larrick
Cover Illustration: Jerry Cowart

To order books: Call 1-866-Words Can Heal (1-866-967-3722)
          E-mail books@wordscanheal.org
          See http://www.wordscanheal.org

To our
spouses and children,
whose kind words and support
made this book possible

Acknowledgments

Thank you to the following people who have contributed directly to the creation of this book: Gavriella Aber, Y. Appel, Shimon Apisdorf, Sara Averick, Michelle Chandler, Bob Citron, Cynthia Citron, Kirk Citron, Rick Citron, Donna Cohen, Gerald Engelhart, Robert & Judy Feld, Erica Goldberg, Mimi Jankovitz, Nadine Kochavi, Elizabeth Kraft, Shirley Lebovics, Nancy Leeser, David Lieberman, Liora Lurie, Jennifer Laszlo Mizrahi, Zelig Pliskin, Eva Rich, Harvey Rich, Dena Samuels, Nachum Sauer, Robin Shoen, Devorah Miriam Tarkieltaub, Florence Taylor, R. N. Weinberg, and many others too numerous to mention.

Thank you also to all the people of vision who have made not only this book but the entire Words Can Heal campaign possible. A special thanks to David Suissa of Suissa Miller Advertising.

About the Authors

Hilary Rich is the author of several books including *The Complete Idiot's Guide To The Perfect Marriage* and *How To Be A Great Catch*.

Irwin Katsof is the author of *How To Get Your Prayers Answered* and, with Larry King, *Powerful Prayers*. He has lectured extensively and has appeared on many national media shows. He is the executive director of the Jerusalem Fund of Aish HaTorah.

Chaim Feld has been lecturing on the topic of ethical speech for seventeen years. He and Irwin Katsof are co-directors of the national Words Can Heal.Org campaign.

Foreword

The authors of this book strike me as doers, out to change the world – to make it truly a kinder, gentler place by educating toward core values. This book, part of the nationwide Words Can Heal initiative, is an amazing project. I am honored to be associated with it.

As an author, I am acutely sensitive to the power of words. I believe the ability to communicate in spoken and written form is a gift from on high. Our job is to take advantage of the gift and not abuse the privilege.

When working on the *Chicken Soup for the Soul* series, I am often struck by the positive power of a good word spoken at just the right time. Encouragement, inspiration, and support to turn one's life around, to try harder, or to achieve the next goal might come from a family member, clergy person, or teacher; it could also come from a business colleague or classmate, even a stranger. By thinking and speaking well of others, each of us becomes the catalyst for feeling good about ourselves, fostering joy in someone else, and promoting amazing achievements in our society.

Unfortunately, the opposite is also true – accentuate the negative about others, tell them something negative to their face, or gossip about them, and you've got yourself one destructive, hurtful, mean, unhappy formula. Spread a bad word – even if it's true – and you demean and diminish individuals and communities.

That's why this book has such tremendous potential: It offers a how-to guide for watching our mouths and our ears. It's certainly a challenge. The authors emphasize that we've got to take it one day at a time. Once we all learn the value of ethical speech and practice it, the prize will be improved relationships – in our personal lives and throughout our country.

Jack Canfield
Author, *Chicken Soup for the Soul* series

Contents

Quite simply,

what you say

is the single

biggest factor

that determines

your happiness

in life.

chapter 1

Life is not a sitcom

Here we are at the start of a new century. Everyone is attached to pagers, palmtops, and wireless e-mail. We spend half our lives talking on the telephone.

Yet, with this worldwide communications explosion, has there been any improvement in the quality of our interactions? Have we learned to use our words to bring people close to us and to intensify our joy of life?

In an age when communication technology is at an all-time high, interpersonal relationships are at an all-time low. The book you are holding is designed to reverse this trend.

Quite simply, what you say is the single biggest factor that determines your happiness in life. If you speak kind words, you will be surrounded by people who love you. If you speak damaging words, you will have strained relationships.

Our society's sitcom mentality encourages us to belittle, embarrass, and behave cruelly to one another because the worst human behavior is the most entertaining.

Words – so innocent and powerless as they are, as standing in a dictionary, how potent for good and evil they become in the hands of one who knows how to combine them.

- Nathaniel Hawthorne

Ultimately, however, we all suffer the consequences in the form of ruined relationships.

In order to begin to create healthy relationships that are filled with trust, the first hurdle we must clear is to realize the power of words. We speak without thinking and have no idea that we are causing our own unhappiness, our own loneliness. We damage ourselves, as well as others, without realizing it. But even worse, we don't take advantage of the most powerful tool we have to get what we want out of life: our words.

> *In an age when communication technology is at an all-time high, interpersonal relationships are at an all-time low.*

Millie

It was going to be one of the happiest days of eight-year-old Millie's life – today she was going swimming for the first time. Millie had grown up in a broken-down tenement on a street without a single tree and had only seen swimming pools on TV. Because of the generosity of a stranger, this year she was able to go away to camp out in the country, and today was the day she had spent months dreaming about.

Millie's bunkmates had already rushed down to the pool; it was hot and sticky, and they didn't waste any time. Millie carefully pulled out the old orange bathing suit that her cousin had given her. It was too big, but her mother had taught her to take a hair ribbon and tie up the straps so they wouldn't come down.

Wrapped in a towel, Millie ventured down to the pool in a brand new pair of rubber thongs. The other girls were frolicking in the water, and Millie bolstered her courage to go in through the gate. She pulled off her towel and stood staring at the beautiful pool with its bright blue walls and shimmering water. It was like a dream.

As she held onto the rail, about to put her foot onto the step, she heard someone shouting across the pool. It was the lifeguard.

She yelled at Millie, "Hey, where did you get that ugly bathing suit? At a garage sale for clowns?" Everyone roared with laughter.

The sitcom laugh track had taught all of these children that it is fine to laugh at someone who is being heartlessly ridiculed.

Millie ran back to the bunk and did not go swimming that entire summer, or for the next seven years. To this day, Millie, mother of three, speaks of this incident with great pain.

***Making fun of someone creates anguish
and painful memories. Our relationships suffer
when we care more about getting approval for our wit
than we do about other people.***

Eric

Eric sat on the bench praying that his teammate would strike out.

It was the bottom of the ninth inning, one teammate was on first, and if this teammate also made it to first, then Eric would be up to bat. The fate of the team would be in Eric's hands, and he knew he could not take the pressure.

The boy swung the bat. Strike two! Eric bit his lower lip. Just one more strike and the game would be over. They would be losers, but not because of him.

The pitcher threw the ball squarely over the plate. The boy swung hard and grounded the ball deep into left field. Now there were boys on second and third base. Eric was up.

He wished he could sink into the ground and disappear.

Eric was tall and lanky, with terrible acne and no social skills. No one sat next to him on the bus, and he didn't have a single friend. He even felt as if his parents didn't care about him. His dad had never come to any of the games until today. Of all the games, why did it have to be this one?

Eric stepped up to home plate. He tapped the dirt off the plate. . . anything to delay the inevitable.

The pitcher eyed him with confidence and took two steps in, to intimidate him and show he didn't expect much from Eric. There was laughter in the stands.

The pitcher wound up and threw the ball in for a clean strike.

Eric knew it. It was inescapable. No wonder his father didn't come to the games. Just as he had said, Eric wasn't worth watching.

Pitch two came in. . . a ball. Lucky break.

Eric choked up on the bat and took a deep breath.

The umpire called a strike before Eric even realized that the pitch was coming.

Now it was the moment of truth. Would Eric be a loser for the rest of his life or have one proud moment he could savor forever?

The pitcher played it for all it was worth. He adjusted his cap. He tossed the ball to his glove and loosened up his arms.

He eyed Eric. The killer look. He wound up and threw.

Strike three. Eric's head fell, and he dropped the bat onto the ground. The boys from the other team let out yelps and clapped each other's backs as they ran in. Eric's team walked right by him as if he didn't exist.

In telling this story, Eric, now a fifty-eight-year-old recovering

> *We never know all the circumstances of other people's lives. If we paused to consider how much pain others might be in, we would never speak meanly to anyone.*

alcoholic, said that he could have survived all that. But what happened next is what sent him on a destructive tailspin that lasted for most of his life.

His father came down from the stands and, in front of everyone there, shouted, "Anybody know where they take returns on rejects?"

Long after his dad died, the words that he had spoken some forty years earlier still caused Eric pain.

It was not just this incident that ruined Eric's self-esteem, but it typified what his childhood was like. He grew up on the tired refrains of "You're worthless, you'll never amount to anything, you're a good-for-nothing." These words became Eric's reality.

> *If you say as many kind words as you can in the course of a day, you will nurture everyone around you and be much loved.*

If you find yourself about to say something cruel, remember that the words you say in a fit of anger will last a lifetime.

Lisa

Fran was standing on a street corner consoling Lisa, who had just lost a baby in the sixth month of pregnancy. Saying goodbye to Fran, the still-distraught Lisa stepped off the curb too early, causing a passing car to swerve. The irritated driver shrieked at her, "Get off the road, you fat pig!"

Lisa sobbed into Fran's arms for what seemed like hours.

Harsh words from a stranger can really hurt.
They give us the feeling that the whole world is against us.
How beautiful it is to spread joy instead of pain
by simply biting your tongue and maybe even
saying something nice.

When we refrain from speaking cruelly, those around us benefit, and our self-esteem also skyrockets because we feel better about ourselves. All it takes is determination to make speaking kind words a habit.

Connie

Connie walked down the aisle smiling for the camera. The wedding was set in a beautiful, flower-filled garden with giant weeping willows in the background. It was a hazy, warm day with a little breeze – just perfect. The musician was playing a beautiful melody as Connie walked up the steps toward the groom.

There was only one problem. It was not her groom. It was her younger sister's wedding, and Connie was the bridesmaid. Judy always seemed to get everything first.

Our self-esteem often waxes and wanes with the circumstances. Understanding this, we should never insult others, and we must always pay careful attention to the timing of constructive criticism.

At the reception, Connie felt very much the outsider as her sister's friends fussed over the bride. She sat at the head table watching everyone dance, feeling sorry for herself.

Connie felt relieved when Aunt Joan came and sat down in the seat next to her. But then her aunt decided to give her this bit of advice: "Connie, darling, if you would just lose twenty pounds, you would be married too."

So much anguish is caused because we simply do not think about another person's feelings before we speak. Often, in an effort to help someone, we say things that are very cruel. Unasked for advice is better left unsaid.

Michael

Every day, Mrs. Lyle squatted down in front of Michael's desk. First she said good morning to all of the other first graders, and then she had her special time with Michael. She told him he looked nice and that they were going to have a great day today. Perhaps, she encouraged, this would be the day he would say his first word in class.

Michael spoke fine at home. His mother said that he used to have a lisp, but he had grown out of it. She couldn't figure out why Michael had not talked in school for over a year.

Day after day, Mrs. Lyle gained Michael's trust, until one day, as he helped her clean the cupboard, Michael confided the following story: It was late autumn of the year before, and the leaves were falling from the trees. Michael, who still had a lisp then, was running around with all of the other kids on the playground. Suddenly, a squirrel darted down a tree.

> *Just don't laugh. No matter how funny a joke is, if it's at someone else's expense, don't even crack a smile. It may stop the joker from hurting others in the future.*

Michael yelled out, "I thaw a thquirrel!" as he pointed over to the tree.

One of the popular kids stopped in his tracks. "What?" he asked, affecting interest.

"I thaw a thquirrel!" Michael repeated in his innocence.

The popular kid howled with laughter and repeated the sentence again and again.

Soon all the other kids took up the chant, and Michael was mortified.

Those were the last words he uttered in school.

This story has a happy ending only through the loving care of Mrs. Lyle, who took the time to build up Michael's trust. Her patience finally changed the situation. Sadly, there are not enough people like Mrs. Lyle to go around.

There is no deeper wound than humiliation.
The momentary glory we may feel in humiliating
someone is short-lived compared to the
damage we cause.

ʃɦelly

Shelly had just come through a terrible postpartum depression. It had lasted five miserable months. She had been unable to take any medication for it because she was breast-feeding her daughter.

On the day that the clouds just seemed to lift all by themselves, Shelly received an invitation to an office party at her old workplace. Shelly had been a gregarious individual, but in the past year she had withdrawn, not feeling up to interacting with people. But this party seemed the perfect opportunity to get back into the swing of things.

On the night of the party, Shelly changed her outfit five times. Nothing fit anymore, but she wanted to look perfect. Her expectations of the evening were overblown.

When she and her husband arrived at the party, several people greeted them at the door and complimented Shelly on how wonderful she looked. That made her feel great.

Later, she stood talking to a group for a while, feeling a bit awkward. Out of nervousness she began talking about herself. Before she knew it, she

> *If you come from a long line of people who spoke callously to one another, resolve to be the one to break the pattern. You will not only have a better life, but your legacy will last forever.*

found herself telling the group all about her depression, something she had had no intention of doing.

One by one, the people standing in the group excused themselves, one to get a drink, another to get some food, until Shelly was left standing by herself. The color ran from her face as she stood in the middle of the room, alone. Wouldn't someone rescue her?

Just then her husband came over to her. She was relieved, but then she saw his angry face and heard his angry voice as he hollered: "Just because you're a lunatic doesn't mean you have to drag me down with you! What business do you have telling everyone our affairs? Get your coat and get in the car."

Cruelty from the people closest to us stings the most. Yet people feel most at liberty to be merciless with their loved ones. We all need a safe haven, but it takes effort to create one. Start by being careful with your own words, and hope that, in time, those around you will follow.

> *People who feel free to be bad tempered around their families are doing nothing more than indulging in wanton cruelty. They pay the price in terms of lack of closeness and trust in their relationships.*

Roland

At age fifty-nine, Roland was laid off from his accounting job. He was so stunned that he didn't have the heart to tell his family. Instead, he borrowed money from his cousin Andy to pay the bills as he searched in vain to find other employment.

Every morning, Roland got dressed as if he were going to work, but he spent the day searching the want ads. He was certain that he would get a lucky break any day now, and his family would never be the wiser.

The holidays came, and it was time for the annual party at his in-laws' house. The entire clan would be there, as well as dozens of long-time family friends. Roland considered feigning illness, but the inquiries afterward would not be worth it.

On the night of the event, Roland claimed to have an emergency at work and told his family to go ahead without him. He figured that getting there late and leaving early would at least make the event bearable. He had not had one job interview in three months and felt like a complete failure.

When he finally arrived at the party, he felt sick to his stomach. He poured himself a double scotch and sat alone in the corner.

A few minutes later his wife pulled him into a circle of people talking about their latest purchases. Just then, he saw his cousin Andy walking toward him. Roland shuddered with fear. Andy was the only one who knew about his situation.

Andy asked Roland why he didn't return his phone calls. He said loudly, "You better pay me back; you're going to lose your house anyway!"

The whole room went silent. Roland turned beet red and said that he didn't know what Andy was talking about.

Andy shouted, "You know exactly what I'm talking about, you phony! Just because you lost your job doesn't mean I have to suffer. Sell the house, you good-for-nothing!"

All eyes were on Roland. It would sound idiotic to deny what Andy said, so Roland just ran out of the house. He jumped into his car and sped down the street. He was in such a frenzy that he crashed head- on with an oncoming car.

> *Television humor teaches us that it's fine to ridicule people and that feelings don't matter. Maybe it's time to choose a different teacher.*

Words have the power to take a life.
If you think of your mouth as a deadly weapon,
you will be far more careful in times of anger
and frustration. You can never fully know the
quiet pain of the listener or what the consequences
of your words might be.

ſummary

1. *Making fun of someone causes anguish and painful memories.*

2. *If you find yourself about to say something cruel, remember that the words you say in a fit of anger will last a lifetime.*

3. *Harsh words from a stranger can really hurt.*

4. *So much anguish is caused because we simply do not think about another person's feelings before we speak.*

5. *There is no deeper wound than humiliation.*

6. *Cruelty from the people closest to us stings the most.*

7. *Words have the power to take a life. If you think of your mouth as a deadly weapon, you will be far more careful.*

Reckless words pierce like a sword. . .

- King Solomon

Three people are
damaged by gossip:

the gossiper

the listener

the victim

*One simple comment
can travel far, damaging
everyone in its wake.*

chapter 2

Yada Yada Yada

It might seem obvious to you that saying hurtful words or yelling at someone will push that person away from you. But other forms of negative speech are much more subtle. Take gossip, for example.

While we are gossiping, we don't think that we are hurting anyone at all. We are simply engaging in small talk. But innocuous chitchat can far too quickly turn into derogatory speech. This is what makes gossip so dangerous. Precisely because it feels so innocuous, we need to be extremely vigilant. As you will see in this chapter, words can cause a great deal of damage.

What is it about gossip that makes people lean in a little closer to catch every juicy word? Why do people feel the urge to share a scandalous tidbit? It's only human, right?

> *If you haven't got anything nice to say about anybody, come sit next to me.*
>
> *- (name withheld so as not to gossip)*

> *Negative speech is any form of speech (gossip included) that might cause damage such as mental anguish, financial loss, physical pain, tarnished reputation, or the lowering of someone's esteem in others' eyes.*

Some people say that gossip is an important bonding tool for business and social groups. But we have all been hurt by unkind words spoken about us, and we have all seen how derogatory speech and gossip can drive children to revenge and violence. Further, the bond that negative speech creates is a false one. There can be no trust in a relationship based on gossip because both parties fear being each other's next victim. If we gossip, we live a lonely life of deception, in which no one trusts us.

The secret to having a happy social and business life is to be surrounded by people you trust – having friends who will not deride you to others and who will have your best interests at heart. If you choose to be friends with people who don't gossip about others, then you can be reasonably certain that they won't gossip about you. Just remember: those kinds of special people also look for friends who don't gossip, so you need to be a good friend to have a good friend.

In business, there are those who believe that gossip is an important part of the company culture, that being in the loop creates a sense of camaraderie and closeness. Wisecracks, humorous banter, and "friendly" ridiculing of each other may seem to give the office a warm and fuzzy feeling, but just below the surface lies the fear of being the next victim. It is far more valuable for everyone to trust each other than it is to be able to laugh together. Besides, there are many ways to spread humor without putting people down.

Chitchat at the water cooler, where co-workers waste time denigrating others, hurts company productivity. Further, spreading rumors creates a climate of vulnerability that no one can escape. The mental energy needed to protect oneself from slander and ridicule mars everyone's ability to perform optimally. Truly, for business managers, the ultimate competitive advantage

> *The secret to having a happy social and business life is to be surrounded by people you trust.*

is staff members who totally trust each other, a condition only available in a gossip-free environment.

Gossip is not just a simple way to pass the time. It causes grave damage in each instance, without exception. If we want to have great relationships, we have to learn to develop trust and avoid speaking badly of others.

> *For business managers, the ultimate competitive advantage is staff members who totally trust each other, a condition only available in a gossip-free environment.*

Allison & Kevin

Allison hung up the phone. She ran down the stairs and out into the backyard, leaving the door wide open. She didn't care if the cat got out, because her life was falling apart.

What Marcie, her best friend, had just told her was devastating. But it had to be true, since Allison knew that Marcie never lied.

Allison sat under the oak tree, buried her face in her hands, and cried. She was six months pregnant and deeply in love with her husband, Kevin. Until a moment ago, she had believed she was the luckiest woman in the world. Now she knew that it had been too good to be true.

She thought for awhile. It all started to make sense – the late hours, the mysterious phone calls, the strange new expenses Kevin seemed to have.

Now that Marcie had caught him red-handed having lunch with this woman, it could not be denied. Allison cried, full of self-pity.

She heard Kevin's car pull up, but she ignored it, preferring instead to have him race through the house looking for her. Let him think something terrible had happened, she thought to herself.

Kevin finally found her under the tree, puffy eyed and sullen. He tried to put his arm around her, but she pulled away.

Allison had her baby to think about; she had no time to play games. She confronted Kevin directly about what Marcie had seen.

It took less than five minutes for the issue to be resolved. For the past three months, Kevin had been planning a surprise party for Allison's thirtieth birthday with a party planner; it was all set for a week away. He pulled out the party planner's brochure with scribbled notes all over it as proof.

> *It takes your enemy and your friend, working together, to hurt you to the heart; the one to slander you and the other to get the news to you.*
>
> – Mark Twain

Allison was greatly relieved, but the incident truly shook her to the core. She had thought nothing could spoil the trust that she and Kevin had built over three beautiful years of marriage. She was shocked at how easily it had come unraveled and that after all they had been through together, she hadn't been able to give him the benefit of the doubt.

> *We all want others to give us the benefit of the doubt, but we often find it difficult to do so for them.*

> *Before you let your emotions get the best of you, check it out first. Don't believe a rumor unless it's proven to be true.*

As for Marcie, she had seen Kevin having lunch with a woman; she had no proof that he was being unfaithful to Allison. There were many things Marcie could have done instead of calling Allison. She could have forgotten the incident, tried to get definitive proof, or spoken to Kevin privately. Marcie may have thought she was being a good friend, but instead she hurt Allison terribly. Of course, Allison should not have believed Marcie; she should have given Kevin the benefit of the doubt.

If you can remember that there are almost no circumstances when it is acceptable to gossip, you will always know what to do in these types of situations. Usually it will be to refrain from saying anything. And when listening to the gossip of others, always remember not to believe it unless it is proven beyond a shadow of a doubt.

We all have an urge to gossip, particularly when it feels like the information we are conveying can help someone. However, there is usually another side to every story.

A Folktale

A young man spread a false rumor about an old man who lived at the end of his street. Overcome with guilt, he worked up the courage to apologize. He humbly walked to the old man's door and said he was sorry. The wise old man looked at him. He said that he would forgive him, but first he must take a feather pillow to the top of a hill and pop it so that all the feathers spread in the wind. The young man thought it a strange request, but he did as the old man asked. Afterward, he went to report this to the old man and asked for forgiveness again. The old man said that when the young man collected all of the feathers, then he would be forgiven.

Our words, like feathers, get scattered everywhere. The next time you are tempted to pass gossip along, remember that once your words are spoken, they can never be taken back.

Do not repeat anything you will not sign your name to.

– Author Unknown

Ruth Smith & Trina

As Trina sat in the coffee shop, she overheard someone mention that Ruth was getting married to the new lawyer in the office. Thrilled at the news, Trina told everyone within earshot. News traveled fast. Soon Ruth got a phone call of congratulations. Ruth had no idea what the caller was talking about. It turned out that Ruth Webber was marrying the lawyer; Ruth Smith was as single as ever.

A year later, the office manager, Dorothy, had a nephew coming to town. He seemed like a perfect match for still-single Ruth Smith. Dorothy discussed it with the computer specialist, Angie, who nixed the idea. She said she remembered that Ruth had cruelly broken off an engagement before. She wouldn't set her own nephew up with a woman like that.

Angie's words seemed to ring a bell, and Dorothy didn't bother to check whether the information was accurate. Ruth Smith remained single for another two years.

*Even a harmless piece of information
about somebody else, one that seems as if it cannot
possibly cause any damage,* **can.** *There is plenty to
talk about without having to resort to talking about
other people, for good or for ill.*

Remember playing telephone? One person would start off, and by the end of the chain, the message would be completely different. How can we believe gossip knowing how distorted a rumor gets as it goes along the chain?

Taʃha & Laurel

Tasha stood on the playground. She was the new kid in the fourth grade. She had been quite popular in her old school, but now nobody would talk to her. She maneuvered her way over to the swing set where the most popular girl in school, Laurel, sat on a chair, many girls vying for her attention. As Tasha approached, the girls got quiet. Laurel stared at Tasha, but Tasha was not intimidated in the slightest. Laurel asked her harshly what she wanted.

Tasha, acting coy, replied that she knew something very interesting about their teacher, Mrs. Gray. Laurel got out of her seat and walked toward Tasha. In short order, Laurel had sent everyone away so that Tasha could confide a juicy bit of gossip. Tasha was instantly assured membership in the in-group.

Bonding. It is vital to our happiness. But if it's done through gossip, the whole relationship is built on a sham. These two girls were not trusted companions; they

Whoever gossips to you will gossip about you.

– Spanish Proverb

were co-conspirators in a crime against Mrs. Gray. Their artificial feelings of closeness may have made them feel good for the moment, but in reality, they could never trust each other and both of them knew it. They used each other for social gain but had no sense of loyalty to each other. All of this at the tender age of nine.

Our urge to bond is strong, but let the bond be real.
We all have a deep longing to be close to one another;
we simply don't realize that it is our own mouth
that is sabotaging our happiness.

Jamie and Lydia

In the middle of a charity dinner, Jamie ran up to Lydia, who was standing in the hotel lobby. Jamie began a tirade about how angry she was at Felicia for seating her next to people she barely knew. She said that Felicia had also put her own name first in the dinner brochure even though Jamie had done most of the work for the event.

If they don't have an audience, gossipers can't gossip. . .Period.

Lydia, who had worked with Felicia before, knew that she had a tendency to hog the spotlight. Jamie and Lydia swapped stories until Meg came up to them. They shared all of the stories with her.

Just then Felicia walked up and asked if they were enjoying themselves. They all nodded. Felicia turned to get a drink from the bar, and they resumed their discussion. They didn't realize that Felicia could hear every word they said. The women were merciless in their character assassination.

The next day, Lydia got a phone call from the president of the organization. He reported that Felicia had quit, saying that she had never realized how much everyone hated her. Figuring out that Felicia must have overheard them, Lydia told the president everything that had been said about Felicia.

The president set Lydia straight. He explained that he had managed the seating arrangements by himself to make sure that there was one volunteer per table. Furthermore, Felicia's name was first in the brochure because she had done much more work than Jamie had. Jamie hadn't followed through on anything she had promised, leaving Felicia with twice as much work. The president said he had put Felicia's name first against her wishes.

Silence condones gossip.

If you listen to someone

gossip, you are

responsible for its

damage even if you

don't repeat it.

Lydia felt horrible. She realized that she had been wrong to gossip and felt even worse that Felicia had heard it all. She spoke with Jamie and Meg, and the three of them bought Felicia a gift and apologized. Fortunately, Felicia was big enough to forgive them. She came back to volunteer for the organization.

Even if the gossip victim is not within earshot, pretend
he or she is. That will help you to avoid gossiping.
And remember, if we don't listen,
gossipers can't gossip.

Why People Gossip

- *to raise their stature*

- *to show intellectual prowess*

- *to bond with others*

- *to get validation*

- *to show off their wit at another's expense*

- *to cover for their lack of conversational skills*

- *to mitigate jealousy*

- *to vent anger*

- *to get revenge*

- *to impress others that they are in the loop*

Talking comes by nature; silence by wisdom.

– Author Unknown

Bettina & Jim

Bettina and Jim worked in the same machine shop. Bettina mentioned to Jim that it was the floor manager's birthday and that they should throw him a little surprise party. Jim got all of the other employees to chip in, bought a card and a cake, and took credit for the idea. At the party itself, the director praised Jim profusely. Bettina got angrier by the minute.

After the party, Bettina confronted Jim about it. He said he remembered the conversation clearly, and he was certain that he had thought of the idea. Rather than giving Jim the benefit of the doubt, that maybe he simply misunderstood their original conversation, Bettina walked away seething.

A week later, a co-worker asked Bettina if he should hire Jim on the weekends for a home repair job. Instead of remaining impartially honest and admitting Jim's capabilities, Bettina used the opportunity to get revenge, and spoke badly of him. She felt totally justified in doing so. As a result, Jim lost the opportunity to work on a lucrative project.

Even if Jim had purposely stolen Bettina's idea, there was no benefit in denigrating Jim. Maybe Jim stole the idea because he was going through a difficult time in his life and needed approval from someone.

If Bettina was too upset to speak well of him, she should have simply said nothing. If she were in his shoes and had made the mistake of taking credit for something, wouldn't she want to be forgiven? If Bettina had decided not to gossip, she would have saved herself a lot of aggravation and would also have made a decision toward more trusting, caring relationships. She then would be able to rise above her grievance and perhaps even act magnanimously.

Feeling justified in speaking badly of others does not make it right. Making a habit of refraining from derogatory speech will make it easier to act kindlier in every way.

The things most people want to know about are usually none of their business.

– George Bernard Shaw

> *The tongue weighs practically nothing, but so few people can hold it.*
>
> – Anonymous

Elaine

Elaine hauled herself up the stairs. The baby was crying again. After so many years of trying to have a third child, Elaine felt awful for not enjoying every minute of it, but nothing seemed to soothe little Tyler, day or night. Elaine hadn't slept much in days.

She picked up the baby and rocked him back and forth in her arms. The phone rang, but Elaine didn't have the strength to get it. She sat down and began to give Tyler his bottle. The phone rang again. Angry at the noise, Elaine kicked shut the door to the baby's room. After taking a long time to finish his bottle, Tyler finally fell asleep in Elaine's arms. She carefully placed him in his crib and fell fast asleep in the chair next to him.

She was awakened when Tyler's older sisters burst into the room crying. Elaine had forgotten to pick them up from school, and one of the teachers had driven them home.

> *Even when you know you're right and are justified in your position, it's still wrong to speak unkindly about someone.*

The teacher, who had to go very far out of her way, had yelled at the children about how irresponsible their mother was. Not only had she forgotten them, but she didn't even answer her phone. As the teacher drove through the traffic and worked herself into an angrier state, she went on, saying that they should not use their mother as an example of how to behave. The children, feeling dejected, never got a chance to explain that their mother had a new baby at home.

People are often the cruelest when they are right. It is very tempting to clobber someone when we know they are wrong. But when we make a mistake, we certainly wish others would be more forgiving.

A gossip is one who talks to you about others; a bore is one who talks to you about himself; and a brilliant conversationalist is one who talks to you about yourself.

– Lisa Kirk

THE TOP TEN TIPS FOR
HEALING with WORDS

- *Bite your tongue before you gossip; your tongue will hurt, but your friends won't.*

- *Stop yourself from gossiping by changing the subject mid-sentence; only you will notice.*

- *Never say derogatory things about yourself; people might agree with you.*

- *Never use humor to put others down; joking around usually comes around.*

- *Speak sweetly, so if you have to eat your words, they won't taste so bad.*

- *The gossip game always takes turns; the only way to avoid being "it" is to stop playing.*

- *Trust makes a friendship; gossip takes it away.*

- *You are the proud owner of a set of ears; use them at your own discretion.*

- *To get friends who won't gossip about you, you must be a friend who won't gossip about them.*

- *Stamp out gossip by voting with your feet; just walk away if someone gossips.*

ʃummary

1. We all have the urge to gossip, but there is usually another side to every story.

2. Our words, like feathers, get scattered everywhere.

3. Even a harmless piece of information can damage someone.

4. Our urge to bond is strong, but let the bond be real. Don't let your mouth sabotage your happiness.

5. Even if the gossip victim is not within earshot, pretend he or she is.

6. Feeling justified in speaking badly of others doesn't make it right.

7. People are often the cruelest when they are right.

Awareness is half the battle. Once you recognize the power of words, you are well on your way to speaking words that uplift rather than tear down.

chapter 3

Treasure Chest

> *It is better to remain silent and be thought a fool than to speak and remove all doubt.*
>
> – Mark Twain

Okay, now we get down to business. Seeing the damage from negative speech and hurtful words is good motivation for change, but what we really need is to know *how* to change!

This chapter gives you tools to help you learn how to use the power of words to create extraordinary relationships. In chapter 4, you can practice these new skills, and then move on to chapter 5 for some inspiring success stories!

You have the power. By changing the words that you speak, you can change your whole life. The wonderful news is: awareness is half the battle. Knowing how powerful your words are, for good or for ill, will help you to think twice before you speak and to say what

> *First work on your heart, then on your skills. When you have the desire to speak words that heal, it will naturally start to happen. Then, to become a master, use the tools and techniques to help your mouth do what your heart wants!*

you mean to say. You will see how avoiding negative forms of speech has a positive impact on all your relationships, both personal and professional.

The future is yours! It's all in the words that you speak!

I. Think Twice

A mother erupts: "Julie! Get in here right now! Did you color on this wall? You good-for-nothing little..."
But if she thought twice, she'd take a deep breath, hand the child a wet dishtowel with which to scrub the wall, and say, "Julie, let's clean this together, and it would be nice if you said I'm sorry."

or...

A shocked wife exclaims: "That's all the money we have left? What kind of husband are you!? You stupid, horrible. . ."
But if she thought twice, she might say, "I need some water," as she leaves the room to cool off.

or...

An employer shouts: "I told you to get that report in by five! What kind of an idiotic failure. . ."
But if he thought twice, he might say instead, "Is there any way you can finish it tonight?"

It is so amazing how, in a heated moment, it seems as if our words have a power of their own. It seems as if we will burst if we don't say what we feel like saying. The shocking news is that if we wait less than five seconds, the potency of the desire to crush somebody usually passes!

You may still be upset about the issue, and still need to discuss it, but what an awesome gift it is that if you just conquer that five-second feeling, you will save so much anguish.

> *That old stand-by, "counting to ten when you're angry," really works. Once said, harsh words can never be taken back, so make it a priority to control your anger.*

> *People often say negative things about themselves: "Oh, I'm such an idiot," or "Figures I'd do that." This is just as bad as if they were saying it about someone else.*

Yelling at someone might get you what you want for the moment, but if you stop to plan what you are going to say, you will have a much better chance of getting what you want both now and in the future. You, and everyone around you, will be much happier.

People often speak badly of others simply because they are angry and venting is the fastest way to relieve their tension. If they managed to keep their anger in check, they would actually get a lot more support from the people around them.

As an alternative to thinking twice, simply walking away is also very effective. With our hectic lifestyles, it actually doesn't come across as rude as it might sound. If you are feeling angry and are about to treat someone cruelly, try to think of something that you have to do right away. This also works if someone is gossiping to you, or if you can't get out of a conversation that you feel is negative or destructive. If you mention an important phone call, a forgotten appointment, or a pot boiling away on the stove, it will seem completely normal to the other person. Even if he or she catches on that you are avoiding the conversation, maybe that's a good lesson to communicate.

2. Give the Benefit Of the Doubt

Instead of:

> *"I can't believe Georgia hung up on me! She doesn't care about anybody but herself!"*

Give the benefit of the doubt:

> *"Georgia hung up on me; maybe I was treating her poorly. Or maybe she's in a bad mood, and my comment was the last straw."*

Instead of:

> *"Juanita took all the leftover food from the party. What a selfish, good-for-nothing. . ."*

Give the benefit of the doubt:

> *"Juanita must have thought that I didn't want the leftover food. I wish she had asked me, but maybe since she has more kids than I do, she's better off with the leftovers anyway."*

Instead of:

> *"My husband stays at work just so he doesn't have to help take care of the household chores."*

Give the benefit of the doubt:

> *"My husband is trying to get us out of debt by working extra hard."*

The wonderful thing about learning to give people the benefit of the doubt is that you actually start to think differently. Instead of spending your time looking for people's faults, you look for ways to see the best in people. That sunny outlook on life will make you a much happier person overall, and your level of aggravation will go down.

Our assumptions about people are often false. Imagine that your friend is an hour late to meet you, so you say derogatory things about her. How will you feel later if you find out she was in a car accident? Giving the benefit of the doubt will help you to think better of others and to act better as well. You also avoid bearing a grudge against someone, saving yourself sorrow and anxiety.

If you are in a situation in which you are forced to listen to gossip, do your best not to believe what is said.

So how do you become someone who gives others the benefit of the doubt? Try to think of five reasons why they might have done what they did. Maybe their actions were not on purpose, maybe their words were quoted out of context, or maybe they had a reason that you don't know about. The next time you think ill of someone, use your imagination. Increasing your sensitivity to others in this way will help you to refrain from negative speech and will help you to be closer to others.

If a friend asks, "Did you hear what so-and-so said about you?" gather your strength and say, "No, but maybe you better not tell me. It'll only make me mad." This will not only give you a better life, but your friend will learn that this kind of negative conversation is not acceptable to you.

3. Don't Judge, Solve

Instead of judging. . .

> *"My daughter Bev is so irresponsible, I don't know how she'll ever hold onto a job."*

Solve. . .

> *"Bev, if you finish your homework on time every night this week, I'll get you that new sweater you've been asking for."*

Instead of judging. . .

> *"Arnie the mechanic is a liar; everyone has the same trouble with him."*

Solve. . .

> *"Arnie, can you please put that in writing? I always worry that if a mechanic doesn't do what he says he will do, then he'll start to lose business. And I want you to stay in business so I can come here!"*

Instead of judging. . .

> *"Fred the doorman is so rude! He barely looks up when I walk in."*

Solve. . .

> *"Hi, Fred! How are you? Do you have to work the late shift again tonight?"*

Instead of judging. . .

> *"My friend Alice is so rich! Her motto is, 'If you've got it, flaunt it.' You'd think she'd use a little restraint."*

Solve. . .

> *"Alice, you have a lot of old clothes. I know a family that would love your hand-me-downs. Would you mind picking out some items for me to take over for them?"*

> *Speaking negatively about others causes you to dislike them. If you need a reason to be nice to someone, think about the fact that you might need him or her in an emergency one day.*

It is a rather enjoyable pastime to sit and judge people all day. It certainly makes us feel better about ourselves. But if we need to put others down to make ourselves feel good, it says something about our own lack of self-esteem.

The best way to raise our self-esteem is not by putting others down, but by doing kind things for people. So rather than judge others, we should try to solve the problem we are complaining about. It will help other people as well as raise our own self-esteem.

It's much easier to judge others than it is to take action to solve the problem we are complaining about. One way to overcome the urge to judge others is to think how we'd feel if someone said the same thing about us. When we find ourselves about to speak badly about someone's behavior, we should first consider how we could solve the problem. The next step is to make a plan and act on it.

The great thing about this strategy is that it puts our complaining in perspective. It's pretty hard to gleefully continue judging others when we know that we should either do something to solve the problem or just keep quiet.

4. Avoid Gossipy Situations

"Excuse me, I need to freshen up my drink."
"I just can't make it to the cafeteria for lunch today."
"I can't talk on the phone right now."
"I'd love to join you, but I have to get some work done."
"I'm going to be late for an appointment; I'll see you later."

When it's you against the crowd, the crowd usually wins. Best solution: Ditch out. If you're not there, you can't gossip, and you can't hear their gossip either!

Sometimes we know in advance that a group of friends is going to engage in one big gossip session. They may not intend to gossip maliciously; it might just be ignorance of the damage that negative speech causes. But we don't have to subject ourselves to it. If we fear that being absent will cause the group to talk about us, we have to consider if these are the kind of friends we want.

> *If someone asks you, "Did you hear about so-and-so?" don't wait to hear what he or she has to say. Reply, "No, but maybe it's better if I don't."*

5. Ask, "At Whose Expense?"

"Yeah, right – let's get Vern to fix the computer; he can't even find his way out of his car!"

When you're joking around, ask yourself, "At whose expense?" Then just don't say it. Find another way to be amusing that doesn't ridicule someone.

"If hanging around at Devon's place is your idea of fun, you need to get a life."

Many people are cavalier about other people's feelings and then they wonder why they are lonely.

"You don't need a ride to the party; you can just roll there!"

Before you say something mean, ask yourself how you would like it if someone said that to you.

"You should have seen how pathetic Janet was! Her hair was a mess, her suit had a stain on it. What a sight!"

Ask, "At whose expense?" What is gained by your comment? Poor Janet, who was having a bad day as it was, now also has two people who think ill of her. What if Janet were your sister? Or you?

There is no law that says you have to amuse people all the time. In fact, if you've set up your life so that everyone expects you to be a stand-up comic everywhere you go, what a stressful life you must have! Get out of such circumstances by finding new friends or by telling everyone you're going on an insult diet. If you can think of something interesting to say, great. If not, just keep quiet.

Humor might seem to be the oil that keeps social interaction humming. But it certainly has the potential to cause great damage. The problem is that humor is often at someone else's expense.

Put-downs and wisecracks might be amusing at the time, but these cutting remarks are not forgotten. The victims will often lie awake going over the scene in their minds, trying to figure out what they could have done differently, how they can avoid provoking that kind of comment again, and how they will get over the embarrassment they feel. This is true suffering – being tortured by the thoughtlessness of "trusted" friends.

> *A broken bone can heal, but the wound a word opens can fester forever.*
>
> – Jessamyn West

> *Being the life of the party might be enjoyable, but if the humor is at someone else's expense, you're hurting your social life more than you think. Everyone might laugh at your put-downs, but they may not be there for you when you really need a friend.*

The three secrets of understanding your intent.

Ask yourself:

- *Am I saying this for a constructive purpose?*

- *Do I have any ulterior motives for saying this?*

- *Am I exaggerating or making the issue seem worse in order to add drama and excitement to an otherwise dull story?*

When a potential business partnership or marriage is involved, it is perfectly acceptable to divulge negative information in order to prevent someone from being damaged. Just make sure you have your facts straight and don't exaggerate.

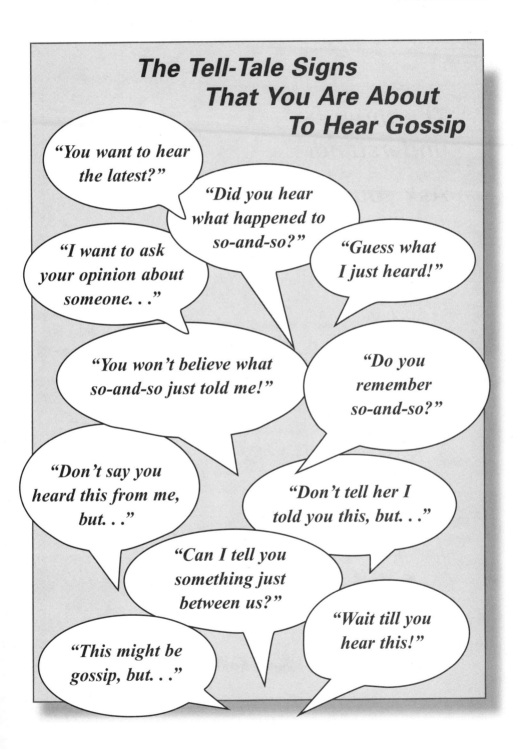

6. Say "Someone"

Instead of:

> *"At the cookout, Meredith was so rude to me. She said my tuna dip was too salty and my pasta salad was nothing special."*

Say. . .

> *"Someone at the cookout was so rude to me. They said my tuna dip was too salty and my pasta salad was nothing special."*

This tool will help you to get the sympathy that you need without saying anything damaging against Meredith. Maybe Meredith isn't kind, or maybe she was simply in a bad mood. In either case, spreading gossip about her is damaging.

Instead of. . .

> *"Chuck parked his car behind mine and then refused to move it! I was so angry and frustrated, and then Lou came along and said it was my fault for trying to get the best parking space. I could have screamed!"*

Say. . .

> *"Someone parked their car behind mine and then refused to move it! I was so angry and frustrated, and then someone else came along and said it was my fault for trying to get the best parking space. I could have screamed!"*

Instead of. . .

> *"Terry got caught cheating on the test!"*

Say. . .

> *"Someone in my class got caught cheating on the test."*

The beauty of the word "someone" is that you can vent your frustrations without resorting to gossip. The listener can still help you with a problem or make you feel supported without knowing the identity of the perpetrator.

It is often valuable to use real-life examples to teach people, especially children, about human behavior. By using the word "someone," you can explain and create examples without hurting anyone.

When saying "someone," you have to be careful that you conceal the person's identity. If there's only one cashier at the corner store, saying, "Someone who works at the corner store is an idiot," will not accomplish anything positive. It will be obvious whom you mean.

You will find this simple technique to be a life-saver. It allows you to vent and to get support and advice without causing any damage.

> *In a dangerous situation, it is crucial that children know that they must tell a parent what is going on right away. This is not gossip!*

> *The secret to knowing whether an incident that happened to you should be retold or not is to ask yourself honestly: Am I saying this to hurt someone, or to get sympathy or advice?*

7. Change the subject

It is just as bad to listen to gossip as it is to engage in it. By listening, we are conspirators in the crime – indeed, it is as if we are causing the speaker to gossip. Not only that, but the gossiper thinks that speaking negatively of others is fine and will continue gossiping to other people as well. We share the blame for the damage that the gossip causes whether we repeat it or not. Just because it is socially acceptable to gossip does not make it right. It just makes it harder to do the right thing.

To stop people from talking negatively to you, simply change the subject. Changing the subject works even if you are the one in the middle of gossiping. Just interrupt yourself and start talking about something else. Here are some examples of changing the subject:

> *In a therapist's office, everything you say*
>
> *is totally confidential so there is no*
>
> *concern that what you tell your therapist is*
>
> *considered gossip. The therapist is trying*
>
> *to help you with the situation, not cause*
>
> *damage with the information.*

We always want other people to understand us and to put themselves in our shoes. How about doing it for others?

To stop another from speaking negatively, change the subject. . .

"I just couldn't believe she showed up in that outfit! She looked ridiculous!"

"Speaking of which, did I tell you about the new jacket I bought? It was on sale and. . ."

or...

". . .and then, he came in late and blamed it on me. Can you believe that?"

"I am so sorry that happened to you. Can we talk about something else? This is upsetting to me. How was your trip to the mall?"

To stop yourself from speaking negatively, reconsider. . .

"Did you see how foolish Floyd looked in front of the boss?" Then thinking better of it, "Ah, maybe I'm being too judgmental, I guess it wasn't that bad. By the way, did you read the funny e-mail Barbara sent out this morning?"

or...

"Do you know what Mary did to me?" Then thinking better of it, "Oh, maybe it would be mean to say; it really wasn't that bad. Let me tell you what Brent gave me for a birthday present. . ."

> *Great minds discuss ideas;*
>
> *Average minds discuss events;*
>
> *Small minds discuss people.*
>
> – Author Unknown

Changing the subject is a very easy solution to avoid saying or listening to derogatory comments. It also appears very natural to the other person, so you won't hurt his or her feelings. Conversations are a potpourri of ideas, with people cutting in and changing the subject constantly. Even if it does feel a bit awkward or obvious, that feeling only lasts a second. The good you will be doing will last a lifetime. As you develop the habit of changing the subject to avoid hurting people, it will become easier, and you will likely inspire others to do likewise.

If you are having a hard time getting someone to change the subject, a foolproof method is to ask him or her an open-ended question about themselves, such as, "Why did you move all the way across the country to come here?" or "What made you decide to become a nurse?" If the person answers your question and then goes back to gossiping, simply ask another question. This method usually works like a charm. It will not only get you off a negative topic but will make the other person happy because of your interest. That is genuine bonding.

**One very valuable way to change the subject
is to defend the gossip victim:**

> *"Every time Sharon comes into the cafeteria, she acts like
> she owns the place."*

Defense:

> *"I don't think that's true. I think Sharon feels self-conscious
> so she acts aloof to make herself feel more confident."*

> *"Cal always shows up late and never gets his work done."*

Defense:

> *"I just think he's a bit of a pinch hitter. When it comes down to
> the wire, I've never seen someone as productive as he can be."*

> *"I never want to see Scott again; he never showed up last night
> and never called."*

Defense:

> *"Before you jump to conclusions, first find out why he didn't
> call. Maybe he forgot or got caught up in an emergency."*

The beauty of this technique is that one of the main satisfactions the gossiper gets from gossiping is that the listener says, "Oh, you are so right." But if you defend the person every time, the gossiper will soon stop gossiping to you.

Defending a gossip victim is a sure way to deter future would-be gossipers from gossiping to you. What an enjoyable workday you'd have without being distracted all day listening to other people talk badly about others.

By avoiding gossip, you might feel that you will be left out of the loop. But if being in the loop means having to torture innocent victims and lose the trust of everyone around you, being in the loop isn't all it's cracked up to be. And when someone needs real advice and a real friend, people will turn to you because they know they can trust you not to gossip. You will be able to help people behind the scenes and form genuine bonds.

Now you have a host of strategies to use to avoid negative speech. This is not an exhaustive list, and it's great if you can think of more techniques as well. The key is to have many tools up your sleeve so they are there when you need them.

Advance planning of what you will say and do when someone starts speaking negatively about other people will increase your success rate. Over time, the less gossip you say and listen to, the better your relationships will be.

If you gossip about others, how do you repair the damage? By asking their forgiveness, which is not very easy to do. Hopefully, if you always remember that you have to ask forgiveness, it will help you to stop gossiping before you start!

ſummary

1. Think twice.

2. Give the benefit of the doubt.

3. Don't judge – solve.

4. Avoid gossipy situations.

5. Ask, "At whose expense?"

6. Say "someone."

7. Change the subject.

The uplifting aspect

of words cannot

be underestimated.

Most highly successful

people will tell you

that someone special

encouraged them

with words.

chapter 4

Work & Home Survival Guide

Part I: At Work

Is behind-the-scenes gossip hurting or helping your company? Does it serve as an unofficial information source, or does it cripple your firm?

The truth is, no matter how helpful gossip might be in keeping people informed, it also creates a hostile environment, destroys teams, and ruins trust. Office gossip is the silent killer of the working world.

If you make the effort to avoid negative speech in the workplace, it won't just make you appear to be a nice person. It will actually give you a competitive edge. Why? Because people will trust you. That is more valuable to a team than any other single quality.

In this chapter you will find stories to help you practice thinking about what to do in various situations.

> *Nobody believes the official spokesman. . . but everybody trusts an unidentified source.*
>
> - Ron Nesen

> *Office gossip is the silent killer of the working world.*

Marty & Ron

> The secret to a fulfilling social and business life is being surrounded by people you trust.

Marty stood listening with the rest of the staff as their boss, Jessica, criticized Ron's report behind his back. Marty felt bad because Ron was his close friend. Ron was in the middle of a messy divorce, which was not public knowledge, and right now he was very distracted.

Marty didn't know what to do, so he just remained silent, but he felt terrible afterward. When he passed Ron in the hallway later that day, he pretended to be in a big rush so he wouldn't have to stop and talk. He felt guilty for betraying his friend.

What could Marty have done differently?

a. Marty could have asked Jessica to stop criticizing Ron in public.

b. Marty could have told Ron about what Jessica had said about him.

c. Marty could have spoken to Jessica privately afterward.

a. Correcting a gossiper in front of a group will embarrass him or her. Instead, Marty could have shown a lack of interest, or better yet, left the room.

b. If Marty reported back to Ron what Jessica had said about him, it would have hurt Ron's feelings.

c. This is the best answer. Marty could have told Jessica directly that he felt bad when she derided Ron in public. Alternatively, Marty could have indirectly mentioned to Jessica how capable he thinks Ron usually is.

∏orie & ∫haron

Norie, the business manager, discovered that Sharon, the president's secretary, had never sent out the bills to the customers, causing severe cash-flow problems. Norie sat down with Sharon privately to discuss the matter. Sharon became very defensive and said she would get Norie fired for questioning her. Sharon stormed out, leaving Norie in a state of panic.

Norie immediately phoned the president and told him exactly what Sharon had done and that Sharon was on her way over to try to get her fired.

What could Norie have done differently?

a. *Norie could have written an e-mail or memo to her boss explaining the situation.*

b. *Norie could have raced after Sharon and told her to reconsider her position.*

c. *Norie could have called Sharon's best friend and asked her to intervene.*

a. Communicating negative statements in writing is just as bad as engaging in negative speech.

b. This is the best answer. Sharon was angry, but knowing that she was wrong, she was likely bluffing about going to the boss. Norie would probably have been able to fix the situation by calming Sharon down and discussing how to solve the cash-flow problems. If this method didn't work, she should have waited. Her boss wouldn't have fired Norie without hearing her side of the story, and when he heard it, Sharon would have been in even bigger trouble.

c. Telling Sharon's friend would have been spreading the damage.

Luke & Jody

Luke sat in the human resources office, thrilled to be starting his new job. Jody was helping him fill out the paperwork and struck up a conversation with him. Jody told him to watch out because his new boss made a lot of promises that he never kept. She let him know that the secretary was friendly with the CEO, so he shouldn't get on her bad side. Jody also said that the best way to stay out of trouble was to always keep your door shut.

Luke was disheartened; his boss had seemed so decent. All his hopes and dreams were deflated. He thanked Jody for her help and plodded off to his new office.

What could Luke have done differently?

a. *Luke could have stopped Jody as soon as she started gossiping by saying that he appreciated her help, but he preferred to form his own impressions.*

b. *Luke could have interrupted Jody's gossip with questions in order to change the subject.*

c. *Luke could have told his new boss what Jody had said.*

   a. While this would be ideal, it would likely alienate Jody – not the best thing to do on the first day of work.

   b. This is the best answer. Luke should also have resolved to try not to believe any of Jody's gossip.

   c. This would constitute gossip.

Many people spend their lives ruining office morale just for the fun of it. Stay as far away from these negative people as you can.

Jill & ſuſan

Jill called Susan into the store office. This was the third time in a month that the registers hadn't tallied correctly. Susan told Jill that Carlos was to blame. Carlos let cashiers work each other's registers, and on one occasion he had allowed one cashier to count and close out another's cash drawer.

Jill called Carlos in and fired him.

> *Beware: Gossip is a powerful weapon that often tends to blow up without warning.*

What could Susan have done differently?

a. Susan could have told Jill that she didn't want to inform on anyone, but she would try her best to solve the problem.

b. Susan could have blamed several people to save Carlos from getting fired.

c. Susan could have taken the blame for the problem and asked for another chance.

    a. This is the best answer. There is often no need to blame anyone. Managers want solutions, not reasons that things aren't going well. Susan should have called Carlos aside at the first sign of trouble and restated the rules of the store. She then could have monitored the results to make sure the problem was solved. If it was not solved, then Susan could have reported the problem to the boss.

    b. Speaking ill about many people is as bad as speaking ill about one individual.

    c. This would mean that Susan was speaking negatively about herself, as well as lying.

Eileen & Neil

> *Our society values humor above trust. But actually, trust is far more important for healthy relationships and happiness.*

There was a policy against romantic relationships in the office. Eileen and Neil figured that if they were very discreet and didn't let their relationship interfere with their work, no one would pay much attention to the policy.

One weekend, Meg and a date were having dinner at a restaurant and happened to see Eileen and Neil there. By mid-day Monday, everyone in the office knew about the relationship. Eileen and Neil countered Meg's gossip with gossip of their own, making fun of Meg's date, and saying that Meg was drunk. The entire day was steeped in gossip, intrigue, and infighting, and very little work was accomplished.

What could Eileen and Neil have done differently?

a. They could have denied their personal relationship and pretended their meeting was for business.

b. They could have said and done nothing.

c. They could have spoken with Meg at the restaurant and asked her not to say anything.

    a. This would not have seemed believable, nor would it have been true.

    b. This is a viable option. If Eileen and Neil had shown they didn't care, it is probable that no one else would have gotten so wrapped up in their affairs.

    c. This is the best answer. Even if Meg was a mean person, she might have been pleased to be trusted, and it would have been the best way to avoid an unpleasant experience.

Talia

Talia decided that she was no longer going to gossip with everyone all through lunch every day. One day, she ran an errand. On the next day, she sat with someone else. On the third day, one of the people in her clique started a rumor that Talia thought she was too good for everybody.

Talia responded by telling the other co-workers, who were not part of the clique, what the group said about them behind their backs.

What could Talia have done differently?

a. *Talia could have gone back to her friends and acted as if nothing had ever happened.*

b. *Talia could have confronted the person who started the gossip about her and nipped the gossip in the bud.*

c. *Talia could have told only one ally what her clique had said about everyone.*

    a. This would not have helped Talia accomplish her goal of gossiping less.

    b. This is the best answer, since real friendship is based on trust, not on gossip.

    c. Telling one ally would have served no purpose and could have caused just as much damage.

Beware of Rebound Gossip: "He said that about me?

Well, let me tell you about him!" It takes tremendous

strength to not tell your side of the story, but restraint

gains you more respect than lashing back ever could.

At Work Survival Guide Summary

1. Try to avoid listening to gossip by either leaving or asking a question.

2. Think twice before you speak badly of others, even if your gossip is to protect yourself from someone else's gossip about you.

3. Beware of negative people who try to ruin office morale.

4. Try not to blame others, even if it is their fault. Try to help them do better in the future.

5. Try to appeal to a colleague's goodness to keep things confidential in order to avoid potential gossip.

6. Don't be afraid to confront people who gossip about you.

Part 2: At Home Survival Guide

> *A judicious silence is always better than truth spoken without charity.*
>
> – Francis de Sales

> *Every ounce of energy that you spend being kind to your loved ones is an investment in your own happiness.*

People can be cruelest to the ones they love the most. No one plans it that way; it's just that at home we behave in ways that we wouldn't elsewhere.

If people stopped to think about it, they would ideally want to treat their family like royalty. But all too often, economic factors necessitate kindness to the boss and relegate whatever energy is left over to the family. . . not a good setup for success.

Now here's the good news. There is something far more valuable to your loved ones than whether you hang up your clothes, prepare a nice meal, or take out the garbage. There is one thing you can do that will earn the devotion of your family, roommates, and friends: speak kindly to them. Once you start, your life will never be the same.

Dan & Colleen

Dan handed his wife, Colleen, a drink as they talked with a friend. The subject changed to the friend's son's college graduation. Colleen winced and looked away. She had always wanted to earn her BA, but responsibilities of life had intervened.

Dan joked, "Hurts to see somebody get what you never got, eh?"

Colleen turned red with anger and embarrassment. "Well, if you hadn't quit your job, I could have finished my degree, Mr. High-school-drop-out-loser."

What could Colleen have done differently?

   a. Colleen could have turned to her friend and explained why she didn't get her college degree.

   b. Colleen could have bitten her tongue, changed the subject, and then spoken to her husband about his comment in private.

   c. Colleen could have walked out of the room.

   a. Dan's hurtful words would not have been repaired by saving face with a friend. The quicker the uncomfortable conflict is over, the better.

   b. This is the best answer. Colleen should have spoken privately to Dan to let him know how his cutting remark hurt her feelings. Such conversations are best handled calmly, in private, and with the goal of resolving the conflict without hurting the other person's feelings.

   c. This would have made the friend feel very uncomfortable.

> *Being kind when it's hardest is*
>
> *the mark of a great person.*

Kate & Arlene

Kate ran into the living room and yelled to her mother, "Arlene stole my pen set out of my locker!"

Her mother looked at her with anger. "Isn't that the same girl who took your make-up kit last year?"

Kate nodded and got on the phone to tell all of her friends about Arlene's theft.

What could Kate have done differently?

a. Kate could have told her mother about the theft in order to get help, but not phoned all of her friends.

b. Kate could have tried to forget about the pen set. People are more important than things.

c. Kate could have said, "Somebody stole my new pen set out of my locker."

> *If you and your friends give the cold shoulder to someone, it seems to create a bond. But what it really creates is mistrust and fear.*

a. This is one good solution, but not the best.

b. Kate has a right to be upset. People are more important than things, but when we are wronged, it is appropriate to try to rectify the situation.

c. This is the best answer. Getting consoled by her mother was important, but it was not necessary to speak badly of Arlene. If Kate had real proof that Arlene was the thief, then Kate should have confronted her directly and asked her to return it and stop stealing. If the behavior were to continue, Kate should report it to Arlene's parents or to the appropriate people at their school.

Jeremy & Charlene

> *It's amazing what people will do for a laugh. Their few moments of malicious pleasure can hurt someone forever.*

Jeremy and Charlene had been dating for about a month. One afternoon, they went to Charlene's cousin's barbeque. All of her friends were there, and Jeremy felt a little uncomfortable. He came back into the living room with his fourth hot dog and found Charlene laughing with her girlfriends. Because Jeremy was overweight, he had the impression that they were laughing at him.

He gritted his teeth and yelled, "Charlene ain't so pretty either without ten tons of make-up."

What could Jeremy have done differently?

a. Jeremy could have asked to talk to Charlene privately.

b. Jeremy could have sat down and ignored the laughing.

c. Jeremy could have asked what they were laughing about before jumping to conclusions.

a. This is the best answer. In private, he could have told Charlene that her laughing with her friends made him feel bad.

b. Ignoring it wouldn't have made Jeremy's bad feelings go away. That laughter would echo in his ears for a long time.

c. The friends would likely not admit their cruelty, so asking would have been futile.

73

Cloe & Marc

Cloe and Marc were riding bikes in front of the house. Marc, who had just gotten his training wheels off, swerved into Cloe, causing her to crash into a tree. She ran into the house with a bloody knee, screaming, "Marc crashed into me!"

Cloe wailed to her mother at the top of her lungs, and poor Marc, who came running in after her, was frightened by what he had done to his sister. Cloe called him some pretty mean names, and it was a long time before Marc got on his bike again.

What could Cloe have done differently?

a. Cloe could have said, "Somebody crashed into me."

b. Cloe could have recognized that it was an accident and not made Marc feel so badly.

c. Cloe could have refrained from calling him names.

a. This approach is good, but her mother likely knew who Cloe was biking with.

b. This is the best answer. In the heat of the moment, it's hard not to be angry at someone, but Cloe should still be taught that this is the correct behavior to work toward.

c. This is also a good answer. Name-calling only makes a situation worse, and then it takes longer for the damage to heal.

Telling to get help to fix the situation is fine.

Tattling when no help is needed is pure gossip.

> *After a dinner party with friends, many people have a good laugh at everyone's expense. Then they wonder why they feel so lonely.*

Evelyn & Carl

Evelyn and Carl drove home from their friends' dinner party, and Evelyn commented about how terrible the food was. She then said the host's husband looked more bald than ever.

What could Evelyn have done differently?

a. *Evelyn could have tried to appreciate the fact that she has friends at all.*

b. *Evelyn could have called the host and shared some cooking tips with her.*

c. *Evelyn could have refrained from saying anything to her husband, but instead told her out-of-town sister who doesn't even know them.*

   a. This is the best answer. Many people make a habit of insulting their friends to their spouse. One way to rid yourself of this habit is to imagine that your friends are sitting in the room listening to you insult them.

   b. Unasked for advice is almost always a bad idea.

   c. This is a poor second choice, but if Evelyn felt the need to speak badly of others, saying "someone" to her sister would have been better than denigrating her friends to her husband.

Jody & Brian

Jody was graduating from law school, and her brother Brian, who had never finished college, was jealous of her accomplishment. At Jody's graduation, Brian sat in the stands with their father and told him that Jody was too ruthless to ever find a nice husband, and that Jody's friends all seemed to be untrustworthy. The comments ruined their father's enjoyment of the ceremony.

What could Brian have done differently?

a. *Brian could have told his father how wonderful he thought Jody was.*

b. *Brian could have told Jody to her face how he felt about her.*

c. *Brian could have simply kept quiet during the graduation.*

   a. While this would have been nice, Brian was likely feeling too jealous to pull this off sincerely.

   b. This would have certainly crushed Jody. The truth is, Jody didn't need to know Brian's feelings about her on her graduation day.

   c. This is the best answer. Often our jealousies and emotions make us say things we don't mean to say about the people we love.

Why is it that we have the harshest words for those we love the most? If we take the time to think before we speak, we would have a lot less to regret.

At Home /urvival Guide
/ummary

1. *When in doubt, change the subject and talk with your spouse later in private.*

2. *Say "somebody," so you can vent without causing damage.*

3. *Just don't laugh if the joke is at someone else's expense.*

4. *Try not to exaggerate the pain someone causes you. Even if you are right, that is not an excuse to make someone else feel bad.*

5. *Appreciate your friendships, and you will never feel lonely.*

6. *Never underestimate the power of remaining silent.*

There is a distressing

lack of compliments

in the world.

Don't just eliminate

negative speech.

Replace it with

positive words.

ſucceſſ ſtorieſ

Think of what you might accomplish in a single day if you spoke kind words to everyone. Everyone around you would enjoy being with you and you would feel euphoric! It is truly within your power.

> *Kind words can be short and easy to speak, but their echoes are truly endless.*
>
> — Mother Teresa

> *Give out compliments all day long. It's the cheapest form of happiness you'll find.*

Rather than complaining about how much others disappoint you, if you focus on the positive and praise them instead, you will enjoy people much more. You will also help them fulfill their potential because they will strive to meet your positive expectations of them. They will be better people because of you, which means they will also disappoint you less.

The behavior of the people around you is very much determined by how you treat them. Wouldn't it be wonderful to be the kind of person who brings out the best in people? You don't have to wait. You can start now.

79

Ken & Marla

> *Maybe if people wore signs saying, "Fragile, handle with care," we would all treat each other a little better.*

Ken sat in a coffee shop staring down at his sandwich. He didn't have an appetite, but he knew he had to eat. This had been the worst month of his life. He had been fired from his stock brokerage job when his new boss swept the office clean of slow producers. Ken had been in a slump, but during fifteen years of ups and downs, he had shown that he could always bounce back eventually. The new boss wasn't willing to wait.

Ken sipped his coffee. The café was nearly empty. Marla, the waitress, came over and poured more coffee into Ken's cup. Marla had been serving Ken for ten years, and they knew about each other's lives. Now, as he walked the streets looking for work, he came in every day as if nothing had changed.

Ken had always felt secure, thinking that if he was ever fired, he could make a few phone calls and have another job within a few hours. Now he was shocked at how quickly his friends had cast him off. How sharp was the modern dagger of simply not returning a phone call.

Ken had spent his career making deals on the phone, and now he could not even get a single person to call him. His self-esteem had never been lower in his life.

He bit into his sandwich. Maybe he was just too old. The brokerage houses all wanted inexperienced, cheap, new hires. How they could employ people who had no idea what they were doing baffled Ken, but it seemed to be the trend.

Marla came over to him. "Ken, go sit at that table over there with those two men. I think I just got you a job."

Ken stared at her incredulously. "Are you joking?" he asked.

Marla replied, "No, I overheard them say that these new brokers don't know what they're doing, and that they need someone who really knows how to manage people to come in and take charge."

Ken cracked a smile. "So you thought of me? I've never managed people in my life. I wouldn't even know where to begin!"

"Look Ken. All I know is, for ten years, you've always said kind things to me. You are the only one who asks me how I am, and you're the only one who ever asked to see a picture of my daughter. If there's anyone who knows how to treat people, it's you. I told Jimmy that, too; he's been a customer of mine for years."

Ken looked at her with surprise and appreciation. He glanced at the men in the far booth and realized they were waiting for him. "Jimmy" happened to be James Barron, the head of the largest brokerage firm in town. That day Ken started a whole new career as the firm's manager.

We say kind words to be nice,
but we never know when our kind words
will pay us back tenfold.

Appreciative words are

the most powerful force

for good on earth.

– George Crane

The Williams Family

The Williams family was having a lot of difficulties. Teresa Williams was a single mother, and she had her hands full working as an assistant in a law firm. Her son, Mitch, was one of the best baseball players in his high school, but he was failing math and doing poorly in all of his subjects. His sister, Tara, constantly made fun of his lack of intelligence, and he always wisecracked about her acne. There was no harmony in their family life.

Teresa's law firm had an annual picnic, and it was always a chore to get her children to come, but this year was different. A famous baseball star was a client of the firm, and he had promised to come to the picnic. Mitch was beside himself with excitement. He brought three baseballs to have signed.

The picnic was held in a large municipal park with acres of forest surrounding a huge stretch of lawn where the football field and baseball diamond were located. The baseball star hadn't arrived yet, so Mitch went over to watch the lawyers and staff toss the baseball around.

Suddenly, a woman started screaming. Her five-year-old son, Ben, had wandered off, and she had no idea where he had gone.

Mitch looked in her direction. There was a path going up a hill, but if he were a little boy, he would opt for running through the tall grass. Mitch jumped up and ran into the grass, followed by many of the men. Others went up the path.

Kind words can make all the difference for family harmony–in good times and bad.

They were shouting Ben's name, but there was no answer. Everyone had that sick feeling that occurs when doom seems imminent. There was a stream nearby, and everyone began to fear the worst. They began to run to the stream to look for little Ben.

As they continued searching, it occurred to Mitch that with all the shouting, the only way that Ben wouldn't shout back was if he were injured. Or, he suddenly realized, if Ben was hiding from them. With that thought in mind, Mitch surveyed the area again. There was a large tree just before the tall grass. Mitch ran back by himself and climbed the tree. There sat Ben hiding behind all the full branches, laughing at being caught.

After Ben got a scolding from his mother, everyone went back to the baseball diamond. By then, the baseball star had arrived and had heard the whole story.

He came up to Mitch and said words that Mitch never forgot: "You know, a lot of people have smarts. But who needs smarts if you have common sense? You're going to go far, kid."

Mitch was never the same.

From that day forward, he used whatever skills he had to the best of his ability. He worked harder in school and did better. He had more respect for himself, so Tara gained more respect for him also. She stopped teasing him, and he did likewise. Their family life really improved.

To this day, he credits those encouraging words for making him happy and successful in his life.

***A word of encouragement doesn't cost a dime,
but it can sustain someone for a lifetime.***

To maximize our relationships, we should make other people's feelings one of the primary focuses of our lives.

Eli and Mr. Martin

Mr. Martin gave Eli his first job. He was hired as a stock boy, but work was hard to find in those days, so Eli did whatever Mr. Martin asked of him. Some days that included cleaning out Mr. Martin's garage, running errands, and cleaning the bathrooms in Mr. Martin's house. Eli was treated very poorly, but he needed the money, so he never told anyone.

One time before the holidays, Mr. Martin asked Eli if he wanted to work extra to help stock the holiday merchandise. He said he would make it worth Eli's while. Eli was very excited and worked until midnight for two weeks. When he opened his paycheck, there was just the regular hourly rate. Eli was very upset; he had had the impression that he would be paid double time for the extra hours. Eli complained, but Mr. Martin said that he had never said anything about paying him double time. Eli was crestfallen, but he didn't complain to anyone else. He didn't want to lose his job.

After many years, Eli decided to go into the army. He had the urge to finally tell Mr. Martin off, but he restrained himself. He just figured that no good would come of it.

After the army, Eli came back to his hometown, and Mr. Martin offered him his old job back. Eli felt like laughing in Mr. Martin's face. But he didn't. Instead, he thanked Mr. Martin for the offer and told him that he was moving to the city to pursue his life's dream of owning his own store. Mr. Martin smiled but said nothing.

Ten years later, Eli did own his own store. It was in a good location, and he really knew how to treat customers well. Unfortunately, he operated on such a tight budget that

Kindness is often mistaken for weakness. But remember that kind people have far superior relationships. And they have the pleasure of living with themselves every day.

84

he could never keep enough inventory in stock to run the business properly. He was always running out of things, and his customers were becoming frustrated with shopping there.

One afternoon, Mr. Martin walked into Eli's shop. Eli was thrilled. He hadn't seen Mr. Martin in a decade, and it was a glorious feeling to show Mr. Martin how his errand boy had turned into a successful businessman.

Mr. Martin walked around the shop. Then he said, "You'll be closed in six weeks. You'll never make it with these shelves half empty."

> *The momentary pleasure one gets from venting anger is often replaced by regret. And many times, the damage cannot be undone.*

Eli was crushed. Mr. Martin turned around and walked out the door.

Eli was so angry; he wanted to tell everyone never to set foot in Mr. Martin's store again. He wanted to find a way to get revenge. But he did not do anything. Life was too short to waste his time being angry.

A few days later there was a check in the mail for more money than Eli had ever seen in his life. It was from Mr. Martin. There was an accompanying letter explaining that the money was a loan for Eli to buy more merchandise. If Eli agreed to the loan at the standard interest rate, then he should sign the letter and return it.

Eli was shocked. He had tried to get a loan at several banks, but he had no collateral, no property, and no track record. No one believed in him. Except for the man whom Eli thought was put on earth to make his life miserable.

Eli signed the document and returned it. With the money, he filled his shelves. The business did so well that Eli was able to pay back the loan within six months. Two years later Eli borrowed again from Mr. Martin and opened another store a mile away. By the time Eli retired, he had nine stores, all of which were owned and operated by his extended family.

> *Make it a habit to give people the benefit of the doubt. It's far better for you to think well of them and be proven wrong than the other way around.*

So many times Eli had suppressed his urge to speak negatively about Mr. Martin. If he had made even one negative comment that got back to Mr. Martin, Eli would never have been able to realize his life's dream. Eli taught his children and grandchildren that just a little restraint can pay off well in this world.

The temptation to bad-mouth someone
who has hurt us is great.
But the rewards for refraining are even greater.

Diane & Greta

Greta, the new vice president of sales, called Diane into her office. Diane sat opposite her and they began reviewing the schedule. After a while, Greta turned to Diane and asked her what she thought of Derek. Derek had just recently taken the credit for a report that Diane had worked on. Here was Diane's opportunity for revenge, as well as a chance to bond with Greta.

She took a deep breath, as if to give herself strength to do what she felt was right rather than stooping to bad-mouth Derek. She replied that Derek was very dependable. Greta eyed her suspiciously and asked her if Derek should be promoted; Diane answered that she was not capable of judging.

Then Greta asked about Fay, another person from Diane's department. Fay always came in an hour late, but she really worked hard. Diane said that she was a hard worker. Greta began to ask about a third employee when Diane got up the courage to say that she really did not feel comfortable speaking about the other people in the office. Stunned, Greta went back to reviewing the schedule with her.

When Diane walked out of the office, she felt as if she had blown a chance to get on Greta's good side. Now, she felt, Greta would just get the inside scoop from someone else, and she would be left out of the inner circle. Diane felt that at least she would be able to respect herself for doing the right thing.

Greta didn't call her into her office for the next week. During that time, Diane, who had always been somewhat of a leader in the office, felt as if her clout was diminishing. Greta pulled all the other employees into her office and questioned each one at length about the department.

If we feel intimidated by someone, we might gossip in order to impress the person with our inside knowledge. Our effort is bound to backfire, however, since the impression we are more likely to convey is that we can't be trusted.

And then, late on a Friday afternoon, the perfect time for firing someone, Diane was called into Greta's office. When she arrived, the president of the company was also there. Diane could see the writing on the wall.

They sat her down, and the president said that of the twenty-four people in Diane's department, Diane was the only one who did not speak badly

> *Don't ever stop to wonder if you did the right thing by refraining from gossiping. The answer is always yes. You may not see the positive results directly, but know that good always comes from it.*

about anyone. The president said that someone who cares that much about people would be the best one to lead them. He asked if Diane would consider becoming the new vice president of her department.

Diane stared at Greta in confusion. Greta explained that she had stepped in as interim vice president of sales merely to hire someone from within the department for that position. Greta had actually been hired to be the new vice president of marketing.

Diane did accept the job, and because of her loyalty to her staff, and her zero tolerance for gossip and back-stabbing, Diane built the best sales department the company had ever had. There was high morale, low turnover, and a sense of camaraderie and trust that made working in her department a pleasure.

**The long-term benefits of not speaking
derogatorily about others cannot
be underestimated.**

Rachel & Michelle

Rachel picked up her phone to hear someone screaming at her. Rachel remained silent while the person ranted, realizing it was Michelle, the woman who delivered her newspaper. Apparently Rachel hadn't paid her bill, and Michelle had to advance the money out of her own pocket. Rachel interrupted the shouting and said she would call the newspaper to find out what was going on.

The newspaper apologized for neglecting to send Rachel a bill. They told her that Michelle had indeed advanced sixteen dollars to Rachel's account, but Rachel could just leave a check for Michelle taped to her door the following morning.

Rachel was furious that Michelle hadn't first checked with her own office to figure out what the problem was before screaming at her. She called Michelle to tell her that it was the newspaper's fault, but Michelle simply started screaming at her again. Michelle said that she had children to feed and that Rachel was selfish for not calling the newspaper to ask why her bill never came. Every morning for months she had expected Rachel's check, but it was never there. Rachel's head was spinning, and then Michelle slammed down the phone.

Rachel stood holding the phone in the air. She was dumbstruck. She wanted to call the newspaper and get Michelle fired. But for some reason, she had a pang of sympathy for this poor, mixed-up woman.

> *Anger and haste lead to actions that we may not be proud of. Often we don't have the time or the presence of mind to give someone the benefit of the doubt. But the more we try, the easier it becomes.*

She sat there for several minutes wondering what to do. All this for a lousy sixteen dollars! Then it occurred to her that if Michelle was that upset over sixteen dollars, she must be in pretty horrible financial shape.

Rachel thought of an idea, and suddenly, she felt a kind of elation that she had never felt before. She wrote a check out for twenty-five dollars and left it in an envelope for Michelle. She added a note saying that she was sorry and that she had enclosed a tip for causing Michelle so much trouble.

The next day, Michelle called to apologize to Rachel. Michelle said she was pregnant, and her emotions were totally out of control. She said that her husband was in the hospital, and that she and the kids were on the verge of being kicked out of their apartment. They were desperate for money. Michelle said that when she opened Rachel's letter, the kind words and the check made her feel like the world wasn't such a rotten place after all.

We never know the impact of our words.
Kindness in the face of anger
can produce miracles.

The next time you feel angry, stop and think about how an extraordinary person would behave; then give it a try!

George

George adjusted his tie in the mirror. Going to this luncheon was the hardest thing he had ever had to do. Not many people knew about his business bankruptcy yet, and this important group of entrepreneurs was his best shot to get a job. He would have to take the chance that someone there might know about it and say something embarrassing.

> *It is very hard to undo the damage once you've embarrassed someone. Think carefully before you speak, especially in a public setting.*

George pulled into the circular drive of the hotel. His self-confidence was shot, but he tried to bolster himself as he walked toward the reception area. Everyone stood around in small clusters waiting for the luncheon to begin. His anxiety level peaked as he saw some of the men reading the local paper. He had forgotten to check it.

One man looked up at him and shouted, "Hey George, what happened?"

George pretended not to realize that the man was talking to him.

"George!" the man called out again. "Isn't this your office?" he asked holding up a picture of George's office with the headline "Local Firm Goes Bankrupt." The commotion quieted the room.

George's face turned deep crimson. He stood in the middle of the room, all eyes upon him. This was his worst nightmare.

The man who had yelled to George crumbled the newspaper, horrified at what he had done. He hadn't meant to embarrass George; he was stunned about the news and was just trying to get clarification.

Everyone stood motionless; no one knew what to say or do to break the awful silence.

Then Craig Newman, one of the most prominent businessmen in town, called out, "Hey, George, I went bankrupt three times before I made it. In fact, I've never hired a manager who couldn't tell me about a failure. That's the only way you really learn how to do things right." He came over to George and slapped him on the back. Then he added, "Hey, someone better snap George up quickly. His experience is the best insurance policy that the same thing won't happen to you!"

Craig Newman's kind words saved George at one of the worst moments of his life. The room started buzzing with conversation again, and George got two job leads to follow up on.

__Even when it feels uncomfortable or embarrassing__
__for you to speak up, a kind word can save__
__someone years of anguish.__

Ann & Mrs. Morgan

Ann was a terrible student. She was smart, but she just didn't care. She was eleven years old and had declined in just about every way since her father had left two years earlier. Her mother worked two jobs and didn't get home until eight or sometimes nine at night. Ann had only the TV and a stuffed frog for company.

Down the hallway from Ann lived Mrs. Morgan, known as "the crazy lady in 1F." Mrs. Morgan had been a recluse ever since her son had died five years earlier. She played the piano every afternoon, and Ann made a habit of sitting in the hallway outside her door listening; she didn't care what anyone else thought. It was the most glorious music she had ever heard.

After many weeks, Mrs. Morgan finally let Ann sit on the couch to listen, and Ann was overjoyed. There were piles of piano books everywhere, but Mrs. Morgan hadn't taught anyone in five years.

> *People often prejudge others and lose a*
>
> *wonderful opportunity to be close to them.*

Finally, one day, Mrs. Morgan let Ann sit down on the bench next to her. Ann thought her heart would burst. Mrs. Morgan didn't speak to Ann but simply began playing a lighthearted piece by Mozart. Ann couldn't contain her joy, and tears began flowing down her face. When Mrs. Morgan noticed, she stopped her playing and looked at Ann, and then took Ann by surprise. She put both her arms around Ann, and began weeping.

They sat crying in each other's arms, but slowly, their crying turned into laughter. The two of them laughed the most full-bodied laugh that either of them had in years.

From that day forward, Ann had a lesson with Mrs. Morgan twice a week at no charge. They worked through Bach and Mozart, and Ann proved a natural. Mrs. Morgan's encouraging words were like water to a thirsty plant, and Ann began to blossom. Mrs. Morgan told Ann that dreams really can come true if you're willing to work for them. Those words changed Ann's life.

Ann practiced in Mrs. Morgan's apartment for hours, and her dedication was inspiring. Her schoolwork also improved steadily. Mrs. Morgan's faith in her pupil's abilities spread to all areas of Ann's life. It was a proud moment when a photo of Ann and Mrs. Morgan was placed on the piano. It sat next to the photo of her deceased son.

Then came the sad day when Ann's mother told her that they were moving out of state. Ann cried for hours. On the day they left, Ann sat her frog on the piano to keep Mrs. Morgan company. Mrs. Morgan accepted it with reluctance because she knew how much it meant to Ann. It was the last thing Ann's father had given her.

> *Connecting with others is what makes life worth living.*

Many years passed and Mrs. Morgan took Nathan, her top student, downtown. A prominent university was holding auditions in their city. Mrs. Morgan sat down in the auditorium as Nathan went up on stage to sit at the grand piano.

The professor sat in the first row, a large clipboard in her hand. The audition went very well, and the professor walked Nathan over to Mrs. Morgan to share the good news that he was accepted into the university.

When they got close enough to recognize each other, Ann, the professor, fell onto Mrs. Morgan's shoulder. Again they cried in each other's arms.

When they composed themselves, Mrs. Morgan was the first to speak. "Ann, I don't know how to ever thank you. You gave me my life back."

Ann looked at her, astonished that she was the one being thanked. "No. Thank you," she responded. "You gave me my life."

It's all in the power of words. . .

Epilogue

You have the power to create a beautiful life. It's all in the words that you choose to say or refuse to say. Each day provides new opportunities either to hurt or to heal, and in this way, you create who you are.

The path of healing with words is harder. It takes more thought, more time, and more determination. And it will seem that everyone around you is trying to sabotage your efforts. But your happiness, and the happiness of those around you, depends on the words that you speak. What's it going to be today?

Words Can Heal.Org is a visionary national media and educational campaign designed to promote the value and practice of ethical speech in order to improve our democracy and build mutual respect, honor, and integrity.

Join US Senate Majority Leader Tom Daschle, AOL Time Warner Venture Group President Lennert Leader, Goldie Hawn, Rene Russo, *Chicken Soup for the Soul*'s Jack Canfield, and many others who are active leaders of the initiative. You, too, can play a key role in this ambitious undertaking to improve our society and make a difference in the lives of millions of Americans.

Enhance your interpersonal relations at every level, from the most intimate to the most casual. Seize the initiative and make a difference in your home, school, community, and workplace.

Act now! Order this book, coordinate a seminar, or arrange for a speaker. They're all just a phone call, e-mail, or Web site away.

1-866-Words Can Heal (1-866-967-3722)
books@wordscanheal.org
seminars@wordscanheal.org
www.wordscanheal.org

To share your own story about words, send it to story@wordscanheal.org.

Books are available to schools, places of worship, businesses, and community organizations at special group rates.
Contact groupsales@wordscanheal.org.